P9-EMK-331

Essential Viewpoints

COSMETIC
SURGERY

Essential Viewpoints

COSMETIC SURGERY

BY MARCIA AMIDON LUSTED

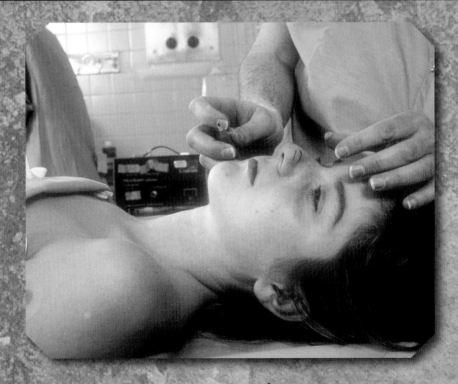

Content Consultant
Joan C. Chrisler, PhD
Professor of Psychology
Connecticut College

ABDO
Publishing Company

CREDITS

Published by ABDO Publishing Company, 8000 West 78th Street, Edina, Minnesota 55439. Copyright © 2010 by Abdo Consulting Group, Inc. International copyrights reserved in all countries. No part of this book may be reproduced in any form without written permission from the publisher. The Essential Library™ is a trademark and logo of ABDO Publishing Company.

Printed in the United States.

Editor: Jill Sherman
Copy Editor: Erika Wittekind
Interior Design and Production: Rebecca Daum
Cover Design: Rebecca Daum

Library of Congress Cataloging-in-Publication Data
Lusted, Marcia Amidon.
  Cosmetic surgery / by Marcia Amidon Lusted.
     p. cm. — (Essential viewpoints)
  Includes bibliographical references and index.
  ISBN 978-1-60453-530-3
  1. Surgery, Plastic—Juvenile literature. I. Title.

  RD119.L87 2009
  617.9'5—dc22

                                       2008034903

TABLE OF CONTENTS

A woman examines herself in a mirror.

AN OBSESSION
WITH LOOKS

On any day, the average U.S. consumer
is exposed to constant messages about
beauty and appearance. Television and magazine
ads tell people that it is important to be attractive.
People are encouraged to buy makeup and clothing,

join weight-loss programs, or ask their doctors to prescribe weight-loss drugs.

Millions of people have also tuned in to television's reality shows, such as *Extreme Makeover* or *The Swan.* In these shows, people who believe they are ugly undergo an intense regimen of cosmetic surgery, dieting, exercise, and other procedures. When they reach the end, they have been transformed into society's version of beauty.

Adults and teens are turning to cosmetic surgical procedures at a greater rate than ever before. According to the American Society for Aesthetic Plastic Surgery, 11.7 million cosmetic surgeries were performed in the United States in 2007. Such surgeries include those to remove fat, to change breast size, and to change facial features. Women most typically have these procedures. A growing number of women are having surgery to change their bodies after pregnancy. But cosmetic surgery is not limited to women alone: men

Reality Television

Reality TV shows about cosmetic surgery, such as *Extreme Makeover, I Want a Famous Face, Dr. 90210,* and *Miami Slice,* became very popular in the early 2000s. However, doctors fear that people who have watched these shows may have unrealistic ideas about what these surgeries really involve. Doctors need to warn patients that the situations that come up in these shows are for entertainment value. The shows do not always reflect what happens in real life.

accounted for 9 percent of all cosmetic surgeries in 2007.

Why are so many people turning to cosmetic surgery? It is often suggested that Americans feel the need to have cosmetic surgery because of pressures from society. Media images on television and in magazines show constant images of beautiful people. According to a reporter for *Psychology Today*, people are more self-conscious about their looks when in the presence of beautiful people:

> It is not that people on television are on average much better-looking than the rest of us, though that is certainly true. It is also that the average American spends four hours a day watching television. It would be surprising if all that viewing time did not make us more self-conscious.[1]

THE HEART OF THE CONTROVERSY

Cosmetic surgery was once something that only the very wealthy or the very famous had. It was also usually done in secrecy. Average people could not afford to have these procedures. And public opinion was generally unfavorable toward cosmetic surgery.

Now, cosmetic surgery is accessible to everyone, as long as they can pay the bill. But has society created an unrealistic image of beauty that emphasizes youth? Many people are no longer happy with their faces and bodies. They do not tolerate the natural signs of aging. Increasingly, people are turning to cosmetic surgeons. Both surgical and noninvasive procedures are popular ways to bring people closer to the ideal body.

Those who favor cosmetic surgery see it as a useful tool to achieve beauty. Others see unnecessary surgery as a drastic and dangerous step. They encourage people to be happy with the features they have.

WHO IS DOING WHAT?

The cosmetic procedures being performed vary

Cultural Values

The definition of beauty changes according to the society that an individual belongs to. Cultural definitions of beauty often reflect traits that are unusual to that culture. Fatness is considered attractive in a culture where few people have enough to eat. Blonde hair was once valued in the darker-skinned, darker-haired Italian people of Venice.

As Deborah Sullivan states in her book *Cosmetic Surgery: The Cutting Edge of Commercial Medicine in America*, "Cosmetic surgery is a modern variation of a practice as old as humankind. Every culture has some customs that prescribe deliberately changing a body's natural appearance."[2] Some customs may seem strange to those not from that culture. Paduang women in Thailand have elongated their necks with metal collars. Chinese women used to bind their feet to keep them small. To another culture, the large breasts and small noses of the "perfect" women in the United States seem just as strange.

Michael Jackson is well known for his many cosmetic surgeries.

by the age, the gender, and the ethnicity of the patient. Among women, the top cosmetic surgeries are breast augmentation, liposuction, eyelid surgery, abdominoplasty (also known as tummy tuck), and breast reduction. For men, liposuction, eyelid surgery, rhinoplasty (also known as a nose job), breast reduction, and hair transplants top the list. Teens under the age of 18 are most likely to have nose jobs. Young women are more likely to have breast surgery. Men are more likely to seek procedures that will make them look younger and more fit so that they can remain competitive in the workplace. Women have procedures to help them appear younger and more attractive. Teens may seek surgery to correct features that others make fun of.

Ethnic and cultural expectations may also influence whether someone has a cosmetic procedure. Some people will have surgery to appear less ethnic. They may want to achieve the American standard of beauty. Some Asian women have had eyelid surgery to make their eyes appear larger and rounder. Some Jewish Americans and African Americans change the shape of their noses so they are smaller and narrower.

Benefits of Cosmetic Surgery

There are many positive aspects to the availability of cosmetic surgical procedures. The ability to correct

Michael Jackson

One of the most famous and most visible examples of a celebrity who has had a great deal of cosmetic surgery is Michael Jackson. It is rumored that he has had as many as ten cosmetic procedures done on his nose alone. He has also had his chin and eyes reshaped, his eyebrows tattooed, and his skin lightened.

birth defects, burns, and injuries helps improve a person's self-image. In addition, people can change physical features that make them feel self-conscious. Cosmetic surgery is often seen as another tool that people can utilize to help them feel more attractive and confident. As Bethanne Snodgrass comments in *The Makeover Myth*,

> Cosmetic interventions are about normalizing—that is, striving to achieve the current cultural norms of appearance. They are also promoted as ways to restore or obtain beauty, youth, sex appeal, status, and happiness.[3]

The American Society for Aesthetic Plastic Surgery (ASAPS) supports patients who choose to have cosmetic procedures. The organization encourages patients to become educated about their options. ASAPS also promotes high standards among doctors. Through research,

Joan Rivers

In 2004, Joan Rivers, a celebrity well known for her many cosmetic surgeries, appeared on a TV drama about cosmetic surgeons. In the show, her character asks to be restored to the woman she would have been if she had not had multiple cosmetic procedures. After she is shown a computer simulation of what she might look like today, she changes her mind.

ASAPS keeps patients and doctors up-to-date with the best information and safest techniques.

DRAWBACKS OF COSMETIC SURGERY

Others feel that the increasing number of cosmetic surgical procedures are leading in a dangerous direction. Critics do not think that personal fulfillment should be closely linked to physical perfection. Fulfillment, they say, can be found through spirituality, art, nature, love, learning, and other activities. The more devoted society becomes to physical looks, the more difficult it is for regular people who may feel that they do not measure up. As author Christine Rosen notes in her article "The Democratization of Beauty,"

> *Cosmetic surgery might make individual people happier, but in the aggregate it makes life worse for everyone . . . the pressure to conform to these elevated standards increases. So, too, does the amount of time and money we spend on what is ultimately a futile goal: cheating time.*[4]

In addition, the health risks related to cosmetic surgery are great. In some cases, these procedures have resulted in permanent disfigurement and even death.

The Love Your Body Foundation is one organization that does not approve of routine or unnecessary cosmetic surgery. This organization encourages women to have a healthy body image so that they will not consider risky surgery. If women are happy with the bodies they have, the need for cosmetic surgery may one day disappear.

The decision for those thinking about having cosmetic surgery rests in their individual reasons and expectations for having the surgery. But no one should make this decision lightly. All aspects of surgery need to be explored for an individual to understand the risks, the consequences, and the value of these procedures. For some people, cosmetic surgery will transform their lives. But for others, it is an unnecessary and dangerous option.

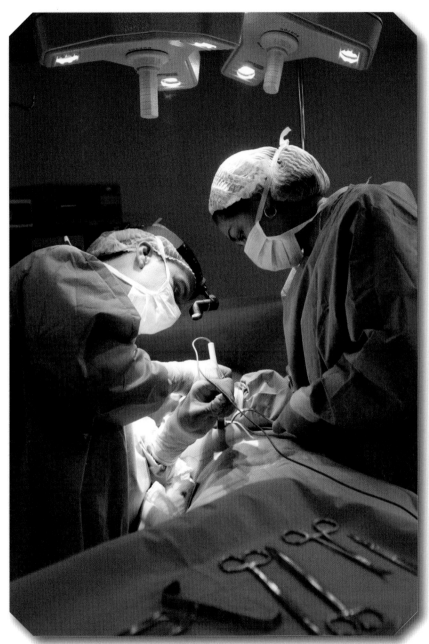

Cosmetic surgery gains popularity every year.

Fanny Brice had a nose job in 1923.

THE EVOLUTION OF COSMETIC SURGERY

In 1923, a Jewish actress and comedian named Fanny Brice had a surgical procedure commonly called a nose job to make her nose smaller. Today, nose jobs are one of the most common cosmetic surgery procedures. But Brice's operation was news because she was one of the first celebrities to publicly admit to plastic surgery. Until that time, procedures such as this were kept secret. When asked why she had the operation, Brice said it was so that she would be more versatile as an actress. Brice had brought cosmetic surgery into the open and helped launch a new era in how it was perceived. She used it to improve her looks and her career. Her public admission helped strip away the old taboos about "beauty surgery."

From Tattoos to Cheek Flaps

Even in 1923, the idea of changing one's looks purposely, according to cultural ideals of beauty, was not a new one. Throughout time, cultures have resorted to various methods to enhance beauty. This included tattooing, tooth blackening, scarring, lip plates, teeth filed to sharp points, elongated necks, and the tiny bound feet of Chinese women. These beauty practices may seem strange to those who are not part of these cultures. But these were

Fanny's Nose

Actress Fanny Brice's decision to have her nose reshaped in 1923 was controversial. Most people felt that the Jewish actress wanted to make her face look less Jewish. Writer Dorothy Parker, known for her witty comments, said that Brice had "cut off her nose to spite her race."[1]

normal and accepted attributes of beauty for those cultures.

In addition, reconstructive surgery has existed for thousands of years. As early as 600 BCE, a Hindu surgeon was able to reconstruct a missing nose using a flap of skin from the patient's cheek. The Romans were able to perform simple procedures, such as repairing ears that had been stretched or damaged. Around 1000 CE, it was common for warriors to slash off the upper lips and noses of their enemies. Surgeons had methods for rebuilding these missing parts from flaps of neck skin.

Before anesthesia and pain medication were perfected, any surgical procedure was very painful and would not be done for cosmetic reasons alone. With a poor understanding of sterilization and few disinfectants available, infections were common. Once sterile techniques, antibiotics, and anesthesia were discovered, elective surgery became possible.

Defining Plastic Surgery

When World War I ended, doctors met to define a new specialty known as plastic surgery. They used the term "plastic" to represent the process of creating or forming new body structures to replace missing parts. The word "plastic" comes from the Greek word "plastikos," is an adjective meaning formed or molded. Eventually the term "plastic surgeon" replaced the older term "beauty doctor" for those who practiced cosmetic surgery.

Advancements in plastic surgery came through reconstructive surgery in World War I.

Cosmetic Surgery from the Trenches

World War I (1914–1918) had the greatest effect on modern cosmetic surgery knowledge and techniques. The development of trench warfare and the use of more powerful weapons resulted in damaging facial injuries. The deep and messy wounds that surgeons and doctors were treating led them to create new procedures to repair the damage. According to Sullivan in *Cosmetic Surgery*,

As [the doctors] sought to restore function, they also tried to create an appearance that would allow a veteran to return to his family and his work . . . Most of the injured were willing to undergo virtually any ordeal, no matter how painful, to achieve this goal. [2]

World War I Masks

Even with the progress in reconstructive facial surgery during World War I, there were still some disfigured men whose looks could not be restored through surgery.

Artists Derwent Wood and Anna Coleman Ladd became known for creating lifelike full face or partial face masks for these men to wear. Using photographs taken before the war, these artists created masks cast from copper. They then painted the masks with oil paints. The masks even had mustaches and whiskers of copper wire, sturdy enough to be pulled and twirled. The masks numbered in the hundreds. Soldiers whose faces could not be surgically repaired were able to move through the world normally thanks to the masks. Derwent Wood said of his masks,

My work begins where that of the surgeon is completed. When the surgeon has done all he can to restore function, to heal wounds, to support fleshy tissue by bone grafting, I endeavor by means of the skill I happen to possess as a sculptor to make a man's face as near as possible to what it would look like before he was wounded. [3]

The methods developed to repair war injuries helped make plastic surgery a standard profession. It also paved the way for modern cosmetic surgery.

Surgery beyond the Battlefield

Reconstructive surgery also benefited those who suffered from birth defects, such as cleft lips and cleft palates.

Children who might have been shut away because of their looks could have corrective surgery in order to look normal. During the 1920s and 1930s, many of the birth defects that might once have left a person without choices now could be corrected.

Surgery to repair damage from accidents also became more successful. In the decade following the war, burns could be treated with skin grafts. Shattered lower jaws could be rebuilt with bone grafts. Severed fingers and toes could be reattached.

The growing safety of surgical procedures finally made it possible for people to have minor cosmetic surgery to alter their looks. The first surgeries, such as Fanny Brice's, were mostly done on noses. Members of ethnic groups who were often discriminated against, such as Irish and Jewish immigrants to the United States, would have their noses reshaped to look less ethnic.

Paraffin

Paraffin was widely used as filler for reshaping noses in the early 1900s. It could be easily injected into the body. Also, it did not seem to react with the body's chemistry, at least at first. Doctors later discovered that paraffin had some side effects. It often migrated within a patient's body. This was even more common in patients who spent time in the sun. Paraffin was difficult or impossible to extract once it was in the body. Some patients developed cancers because of it. Even after doctors were aware of the side effects, some continued to use paraffin injections.

OPENING THE FLOODGATES

After Fanny Brice had her well-publicized nose job, other celebrities began having equally public procedures. The public became aware of cosmetic surgery and the effect it could have on the average person's looks.

Ugly Girl Contests

One of the darker sides of the new cosmetic surgery industry in the 1920s was the popularity of contests for a surgical makeover. The ugliest woman to enter would be chosen for a makeover. A newspaper or magazine would sponsor the contest with a plastic surgeon. The contests promised to make the winner a beauty with the help of the plastic surgeon's skills. Each day, the newspaper would run a photograph of an ugly woman, along with an article about how her looks had affected her life. Many of these women endured the embarrassment of winning the title of "ugliest woman" for the chance to be beautiful. Ultimately, a winner would be chosen for a surgical makeover. It was, of course, great advertising for the doctor.

In the medical community, there was some debate over the subject of so-called "beauty surgery." Some doctors felt that surgeries should only be done to correct deformities and injuries. Others were more accepting of elective surgeries. Eventually, cosmetic surgery became a normal part of medical practice.

By the mid-twentieth century, as the focus on looks and beauty grew, ordinary people began to look to cosmetic surgery. People linked beauty with success. And cosmetic surgery could make that success possible for anyone. Because of this change in public opinion, the floodgates were opened for modern cosmetic surgery.

Dancer Maria Korda examines her nose after cosmetic surgery in 1961.

A woman in China walks by an advertisement for breast implants.

COSMETIC SURGERY
EXPLORED

Once surgeons realized that elective surgery could bring in a lot of business, they began advertising their services. Doctors appealed to those who might be insecure about their looks. By linking the advantages of cosmetic surgery to self-esteem, doctors were able to convince some patients that the procedures were not based on vanity alone.

As a result of these kinds of ads, which appeared in the early twentieth century, the number of cosmetic surgery procedures has increased every year. According to the American Society for Aesthetic Plastic Surgery, cosmetic surgery procedures have jumped almost 500 percent from 1997 to 2007. But to understand the trend of cosmetic surgery, it is necessary to understand what types of procedures are considered cosmetic surgery.

RESHAPING THE BODY

Cosmetic procedures can be divided into two categories. The first category includes surface treatments. These are minimally invasive procedures that can be done in a small amount of time. The procedures do not involve surgery in that the doctor does not cut into the patient's body and no real surgical procedure is performed. Laser

Cosmetic Surgery for Pets?

Some consumers have procedures done on their pets. In most cases, these surgeries are necessary for the animal's health. But some are not. For example, neutered dogs can have testicular implants so that they will still look the same as they did before surgery. Pets can have excess fat removed, as well as eye lifts and face-lifts. Owners of show animals may also seek to perfect an animal's ears, teeth, or tail in order to give them a better chance of winning in competition.

hair removal is one such procedure. The second category includes traditional surgical procedures. These require surgery and often must be done with anesthesia in a hospital or clinical setting. These procedures can be grouped by the desired effect.

Body contouring refers to procedures that alter the shape of large areas of the body. Body contouring may be done on the stomach, buttocks, or legs. One such procedure is liposuction. Doctors remove fat from an area of the body through a suction tube. Liposuction can take hours to complete, depending on how large an area is being suctioned. Patients may have bruising and swelling after the surgery. They must wear special compression clothing and limit their activities while they recover.

Another body contouring procedure is abdominoplasty, often called a tummy tuck. Excess skin and sagging abdominal muscles are tightened during a tummy tuck. Women who have been pregnant or people who have lost a lot of weight may have excess drooping skin. They may choose to have this procedure to make their stomachs flatter and tighter. A tummy tuck is one of the most serious cosmetic procedures. It requires general anesthesia and days of hospitalization.

Some body contouring procedures involve adding implants to reshape an area of the body. Implants may be placed in the buttocks, the thighs, the chest, and the calves. Implants are usually made of solid silicone or silicone gel. They are often placed underneath normal muscles. This procedure also requires hospitalization. Implant procedures also have risks. If the implants are not perfectly placed, abnormal body shaping and muscle damage can result.

BREAST SURGERY

Another category of surgical cosmetic procedure is breast surgery. Women may have procedures to make breasts

The Fringes of Cosmetic Surgery

There are other cosmetic procedures that are too radical for most patients.

A procedure known as JewelEye has been performed in the Netherlands. In this procedure, a tiny platinum jewel is implanted within the eye. A piece of jewelry can be seen on the white area of the patient's eye. The JewelEye procedure is not legal outside of the Netherlands. Its long-term health effects are not yet known.

Other unusual procedures are performed on people who call themselves furries. These people modify their bodies to be more like animals, such as a tiger. They may have tattoos of stripes all over their bodies, sharpen their canine teeth to resemble fangs, and have nose, mouth, or ear surgery in order to look more catlike.

In an extreme form of body alteration, people change their identities by willingly becoming amputees. Most doctors will not perform unnecessary amputations. They may risk losing their medical license if they perform these procedures.

Performance Surgery

The Parisian artist Orlan uses cosmetic surgery as her artistic medium. She uses her cosmetic surgeries as performance art. The surgeries are filmed as she has a series of procedures to make her look like famous female icons, such as the Mona Lisa. These surgeries are performed in an operating room decorated with props. Orlan and her surgical team are dressed in costumes. She insists on only local anesthesia so that she is aware and talking during the surgeries. Orlan says that her work is a protest against "the social pressure put on a woman's body."[1]

larger (breast augmentation) using silicone or saline implants. Or they may want to make breasts smaller (breast reduction) by removing excess tissue. Breast reduction is sometimes done to relieve back pain caused by very heavy breasts. There is also a procedure known as a breast lift, in which skin is removed and the breast is reshaped to look younger.

FACIAL PROCEDURES

Cosmetic surgery procedures also include procedures performed on the ears. Ears that protrude can be reshaped to be closer to the skull. This procedure is often done for self-esteem reasons, especially in children. Ears that stick out may be considered a birth defect.

Facial procedures include eyelid surgery to lift sagging eyelids that make the patient look tired or old. Face-lifts involve removing sagging and wrinkled skin on the cheeks and the neck. The procedure also can get rid of deep folds and creases on the face. Sometimes the doctor must make incisions

Artist Orlan has had many cosmetic surgery procedures as part of her artwork.

around the hairline, the ears, or under the chin to tighten skin. Noses and chins are also commonly altered through surgery. Noses are reshaped or made smaller. Chins are enhanced or reduced in size.

Today, most of these procedures have been used extensively. They are considered to be safe when done correctly.

Noninvasive Procedures

Not all cosmetic procedures require surgery, anesthesia, and hospital stays. Doctors have developed new ways to alter looks using less drastic methods. Botox injections are one such procedure. A small amount of botulin is injected into a wrinkle in order to smooth it out. Botulin is poisonous, but a small amount only affects the muscles being treated with the injection. The drug relaxes the muscles and smoothes the related wrinkles for about six months. Another procedure is the injection of fat or collagen to fill creases from below the eyelids to the chin. When fat is used, it comes from another part of the patient's body. Collagen is a cow protein. It does not require patients to donate their own fat for the procedure.

Other procedures require the use of a laser. Lasers are often used to remove excess hair or dark veins in the feet and legs. Laser hair removal requires multiple treatments. But the procedure usually permanently removes almost all of the hair from the area.

These procedures are increasing in popularity because they do not require surgery. The side effects are also minimal.

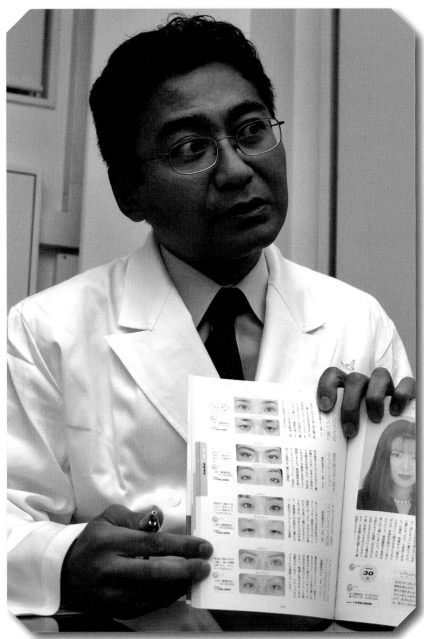

Plastic surgeon Toshiya Handa speaks about current trends in plastic surgery among Japanese youth.

Media images of beauty, such as the Miss America Pageant, contribute to women's expectations of beauty.

THE QUEST FOR BEAUTY

mericans live in a society where people are largely judged by how they look. People who are fat, ugly, or otherwise unattractive often have fewer opportunities for getting good jobs. They may also be discriminated against in other ways.

EXPECTATION OF BEAUTY

Some workers face age discrimination in their jobs. They feel that they need to look younger in order to remain competitive or even employed at all. Women returning to work after years at home raising children may feel the need to look attractive in order to get jobs and compete with younger women.

In the early years of the United States, the cultural expectation of a woman's beauty was based on an ideal of a woman with a tiny waist, full skirts, and white skin. Gradually, the ideal woman evolved into the shorter skirts and hair of the 1920s flapper. In the 1950s, women with more voluptuous bodies, such as Marilyn Monroe, became desirable.

Women today often wear tight, revealing clothing. They are expected to have thin waists, large breasts, and toned muscles. According to Sullivan in *Cosmetic Surgery*, "Modern clothing

Protesting Miss America

The Miss America Pageant began in 1921 as a beauty contest in Atlantic City, New Jersey. The pageant consists of an interview, a talent competition, a swimwear competition, an evening gown competition, and an onstage question and answer.

In 1968 and 1969, feminists protested the Miss America Pageant. The women's liberation movement was gaining strength during this time. Feminists challenged the beauty standards that were being presented. Ratings for the Miss America Pageant fell during the 1960s and 1970s.

Today, the Miss America Pageant is known as a scholarship pageant. Many contestants are awarded college scholarships based on their performance in the pageant.

was far more revealing of the underlying body. . . .
As a result, the physical body . . . became the basis
for the judgments about appearance."[1]

Media

Photographs in newspapers and magazines play
a large role in spreading ideas of beauty. Movies,
television, and advertising increased the role of
the media in defining the perfect body, hair, and
clothing styles for both women and men.

Models and actors represent the current ideas
of beauty and fashion. Magazines, from women's
fashion magazines to men's bodybuilding magazines,
all portray images that many people strive to achieve.
However, many of these images are unrealistic.
Professional hair, makeup, and lighting, along with
computer retouching, mean that most media images
are not attainable.

The media and advertising industries continue to
grow and spread into many aspects of people's lives.
Advertisements line city streets, cover the insides of
buses and cabs, and interrupt Web browsing. It is
becoming more difficult to escape the ideas of beauty
that they put forth.

Surgery on Television

Not only does the media show society's expectations for beauty, but also more and more cosmetic surgery is glamorized in the media.

On reality television shows, such as *Extreme Makeover* and *The Swan*, people are filmed as they undergo a series of makeover procedures. These include surgeries, implants, dental procedures, weight loss, and styling. The procedures are often painful. The whole process can be difficult and embarrassing. Once the people have gone through these dramatic transformations, they are unveiled to

Discrimination

Discrimination in the workplace and in other areas of society, based solely on appearance, is a fact of life for many people. A study in the *American Economics Review* showed that people with below-average looks can earn as much as 9 percent less than their more attractive co-workers.

People are sometimes refused jobs or even fired on the basis of being unattractive. There are often very few consequences for employers who practice this type of discrimination. Employers who would never dare make comments about an employee's race or gender sometimes feel free to comment on their weight, height, or attractiveness. While there are laws against discrimination based on race and gender, no such law exists to prevent discrimination based on looks.

Not only people in the workplace are affected by appearance discrimination. In February of 2007, the DePauw University chapter of the Delta Zeta sorority evicted 23 of its members. This was supposedly done because they were less attractive than the rest of the sisters.

family and friends. The contestants and their loved ones are often thrilled with the results.

There are darker sides to these reality makeover shows as well. MTV produced a show called *I Want a Famous Face*. The show documented men and women who wanted to look more like a celebrity. They had extensive cosmetic surgery in order to have the breasts of a *Playboy* centerfold or a face similar to that of a particular movie star. Sometimes these surgeries did not have positive effects. MTV kept track of former patients and showed viewers that sometimes the surgeries did not make them as happy and fulfilled as they thought they would be.

Like other forms of popular media, these shows serve a purpose by showing what is available for enhancing looks, how it is done, and, in some cases, how painful it can be. They also demonstrate how

The Twilight Zone

One of the most memorable episodes of the 1960s television show *The Twilight Zone* was called "The Eye of the Beholder." In it, a young woman has just had cosmetic surgery to, she hopes, make her look normal. As she waits for the results of her surgery, she learns that if this surgery does not succeed, she will be moved to a special place for people like her. When the woman's bandages are removed, she is revealed as a normal, beautiful woman. But the faces of the doctors and nurses are pig-like and hideous. The surgery failed and she is sent away from mainstream society. The show was a comment on the idea that beauty depends entirely on the culture's concept of normal.

acceptable these procedures have become. According to Bethanne Snodgrass in *The Makeover Myth*:

> The shows certainly appear to have sparked an explosion in interest in cosmetic medicine. Watching someone who could be a neighbor or a co-worker get a makeover has to make a viewer wonder, Why not me? A recent survey of people who had contacted a plastic surgery professional society Web site showed that seeing surgical results on television was a major stimulus for them to investigate surgery for themselves.[2]

Cosmetic surgery is increasing in popularity. A negative stigma is no longer attached to cosmetic surgery. People who had cosmetic surgery in the past were considered vain and frivolous. But now it is often seen as a common way to make a person look better. Also, people in the United States have become more affluent. More people can afford the surgeries.

Barbie and G.I. Joe

Since the Barbie doll first appeared in the 1950s, it has gotten thinner and has larger breasts. If she were a real woman, Barbie would be 5 feet 9 inches (1.8 m) tall and weigh 110 pounds (50 kg). That is far below a healthy weight for that height.

The G.I. Joe action figure has become more muscular. The 1964 version of G.I. Joe had a body that would translate into a man with a 44-inch (112-m) chest and 12-inch (30-cm) bicep, but the 1990s version would be the unrealistic equivalent of a man with a 55-inch (140-cm) chest and 27-inch (69-cm) bicep.

Cosmetic versus Reconstructive

Cosmetic and reconstructive surgery are both part of the plastic surgery specialty. However, they are two different types of surgery. Cosmetic surgery takes anatomical structures that are already healthy, normal, and functioning and reshapes them to improve the patient's looks. It is considered to be elective and is usually not covered by insurance.

Reconstructive surgery, however, is intended to improve both the function and the appearance of body structures. Reconstructive surgery is performed on body parts that are abnormal or damaged. Because it improves the patient's health, most reconstructive surgery is covered by health insurance.

Procedures can be bought at lower prices as more surgeons compete for business.

THE FEMINIST VIEW

The feminist view of cosmetic surgery has been divided in recent years. The cosmetic surgery industry has tried to foster something called "new feminism." It tells women that they are empowered by the ability to choose to have surgery. They are able to take control of their looks. They believe that the ability to choose how they look makes women more powerful. It is another life choice at their disposal, like the choice to eat well and exercise.

Many other feminists, however, argue that this is just a tool of the cosmetic surgery industry to get more women to have these procedures. They advocate that real beauty comes from within, and they worry about the effect of this argument on women who cannot afford to choose surgery.

Locations for Surgery

The business of cosmetic surgery is a growing industry. Unlike surgeries performed because of a medical problem, cosmetic surgery is elective. Patients choose to have it. This means that patients can also decide where and when to have these surgeries done.

Today's consumers have many choices when it comes to cosmetic surgery. They can go to a board-certified physician or surgeon who has been trained in plastic surgery. They can also go to a general doctor who has had some additional, though limited, training in certain procedures.

Consumers may also visit a boutique cosmetic surgery center or a spa. These sites offer procedures such as laser treatments, Botox injections, and other noninvasive treatments. A trained doctor does not always oversee these facilities.

Some consumers also take part in cosmetic surgery tour packages. They go to a foreign country to have cosmetic surgery, usually at a much lower price. But these tour packages often come with greater risk. Doctors in other countries are not held to the same medical standards as doctors in the United States.

Many doctors have been eager to get into cosmetic surgery. In this field, the hours are predictable and the patients are usually healthy. Doctors are advertising their cosmetic services more than ever. It is up to the patient to be a smart consumer with the knowledge to select a reputable doctor.

Cosmetic surgery is becoming an option for more people. New groups of people are having procedures done. This has resulted in one of the biggest controversies in cosmetic medicine to date: teens and cosmetic surgery. ⌐

"In a world in which we are judged by how we appear, the belief that we can change our appearance is liberating. We are what we seem to be and we seem to be what we are."[3]

—*Sander Gilman, author of* Making the Body Beautiful

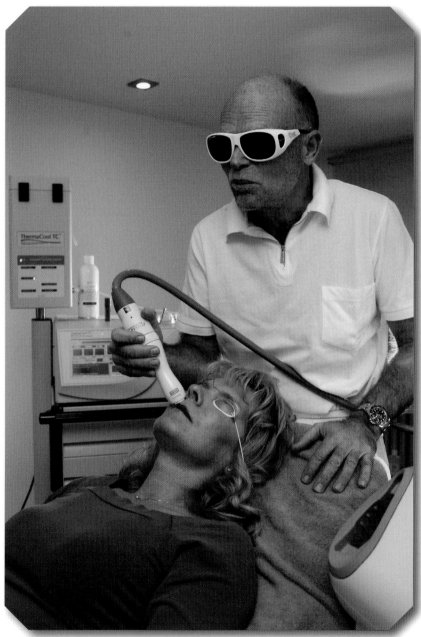

Doctor Michael Krueger uses a laser on a patient at a cosmetic treatment center in Berlin, Germany.

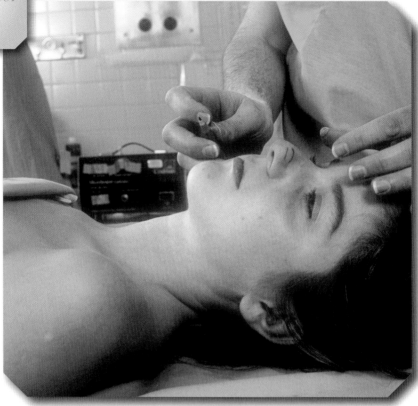

A doctor outlines the nose of a teenage patient prior to cosmetic surgery.

TEENS AND COSMETIC SURGERY

Teens are having cosmetic procedures in increasing numbers every year. Some experts see this as a logical extension in the quest to look better and gain self-esteem. Others are worried that this trend is resulting in many teens having procedures done at too early an age. Teens may not be emotionally prepared for such a change.

A Vulnerable Age

Many people develop and establish their self-image during their teenage years. The way they view themselves can affect their personality, academic performance, and emotions. For many, the way they feel about their looks plays a large role in their self-image.

Peer pressure and social position play a big part in a teenager's life. Looks are important. Teens are often quick to follow fashion tends. They can also be cruel to peers who do not have a certain look. As Bethanne Snodgrass states in *The Makeover Myth*, "Adolescents tend to fixate on visible body parts that fall anywhere outside the 'average.' Typically, noses for boys and breasts and noses for girls receive the most self-scrutiny."[1]

Often, teens are teased for having a big nose, a flat chest, or large ears. As the American Society of Plastic

Any Girl Can Be Good Looking

The push for young women to be as attractive as possible is not a modern phenomenon. In 1927, Hazel Rawson Cades wrote a beauty guide for young women titled *Any Girl Can Be Good Looking*. Cades wrote, "Being good-looking is no longer optional. . . . There is no place in the world for women who are not. Competition is so keen and . . . the world moves so fast that we simply can't afford not to sell ourselves on sight."[2]

Cosmetic Surgery in Teen Magazines

Magazines for teen readers often publish articles about the benefits of having plastic surgery. Matthew Feller of the Center for Media and Public Affairs says, "The press brandishes a double-edged sword. By telling and retelling stories about teens and plastic surgery, they're actually turning into an advertisement for that very thing."[4]

Surgeons states in its briefing paper "Plastic Surgery for Teenagers,"

Teenagers who want to have plastic surgery usually have different motivations and goals from adults. Teens tend to have plastic surgery to fit in with peers, to look similar. Adults tend to have plastic surgery to stand out from others.[3]

Teens are often exposed to media images of beauty through movies, television, celebrities, magazines, and the Internet. Even more than adults, they are aware of their looks. They see examples of how cosmetic procedures can help people change the way they look. Teens know that these procedures are generally acceptable to society. They may believe that by fixing their flaws, their lives will improve.

As a result, teens are having more procedures. In 2007, teens and children under the age of 18 accounted for 2 percent of all cosmetic procedures. Teens and young adults from ages 19 to 34 accounted for 21 percent of all cosmetic procedures. Teens were most likely to have laser hair removal, dermabrasion, chemical skin peels, ear reshaping, and nose jobs.

According to Dr. Darrick Antell, a New York City plastic surgeon,

> *Today's teenagers are growing up with parents who have had cosmetic surgery, so they see and hear about it more. The media has also done a good job of making people aware of the procedures available.*[5]

BEFORE SURGERY

The American Society of Plastic Surgeons has not made a formal statement about whether or not plastic surgery is suitable for teens. However, the organization has developed guidelines to be considered before surgery is performed on patients in this age group. It is important that the surgery is the teen's idea and not something his or her parents have initiated or urged them to do. A doctor should know that the teen wants the surgery and has thought about it for a long time. Teens must also fully understand the benefits and the limitations of having plastic surgery.

Psychological maturity is also important. According to the American Society of Plastic Surgeons,

Teenagers must be able to tolerate the discomfort and temporary disfigurement of a surgical procedure. Plastic surgery is not recommended for teens who are prone to mood swings or erratic behavior, who are abusing drugs and/or alcohol, or who are being treated for clinical depression or other mental illness.[6]

BENEFITS OF TEEN SURGERY

Some groups would like to see a ban on any kind of cosmetic surgery done on teens. Others feel that there are situations in which cosmetic surgery is appropriate for teenagers. A large part of being an adolescent is self-image and self-esteem. If cosmetic surgery can improve a teen's self-image and social life, it may be worth considering. Surgery can make a big difference in a teen's self-esteem. It can also change the way a teen relates to the world and approaches new things.

A young woman named Abigail had a nose job as a high school

Regrets

A young woman named Kacey Long had breast implants at age 19. Several of her friends had gotten implants as high school graduation presents as well. She says that the surgery has brought her many problems. In an interview, Long said that her implants were so big that she "looked like a porn star."[7] In addition, Long experienced shooting pain in her arms, joint pain, and fatigue. She had difficulty getting out of bed. Eventually, she paid for another surgery to have the implants removed. Afterward, her health improved.

Brook Bates had liposuction at age 12.

senior, at age 16. She felt that her surgery made a major difference in her life and was happy with her decision:

> It wasn't an awful nose that people picked on or anything . . .
> If you're heavy, you can lose weight. If you don't like your

hair, you can change the color or cut it. But my nose was something that bothered me and lowered my self-esteem, but that I couldn't personally change.[8]

Many psychologists agree that cosmetic surgery is sometimes a good choice for teens. If teasing about a certain body part is so overwhelming that a person can no longer function normally, then cosmetic surgery may be worth considering.

Negatives of Teen Surgery

Others argue that teens are too young to make decisions about something as important, and potentially dangerous, as surgery. In addition, most teen bodies are still growing and have not yet reached full maturity. As a result, a procedure such as a nose job that looks great at age 16 might look out of proportion by age 25.

Cosmetic surgery for teens has both physical and psychological risks. In all surgeries, there is a danger of negative side effects. Allergic reactions to anesthesia can result in breathing or heart problems, heavy

Breast Tissue Growth in Boys

It is not unusual for teenage boys to develop breast tissue. Most of the time, the extra tissue goes away on its own. However, if it does not, it can be very embarrassing. This tissue development can be caused by hormones or from being overweight.

bleeding, or infection. In addition, the results of the surgery may not be perfect. Everyone has unique facial features and bone structure. Those factors influence the outcome of any cosmetic surgery.

There is also a psychological risk for teens having cosmetic procedures. They may not recognize the limitations of the surgery. The realities of what it can and cannot do for them may not be understood. Surgery can change a part of their bodies that they feel is unattractive. But it does not

Jenna Franklin

In 2001, a 15-year-old British girl named Jenna Franklin made the headlines throughout the world. Her parents had agreed to pay for her to have breast implants. It has since become common for parents to buy their daughters cosmetic surgery procedures. However, Jenna's was the first case to get media attention. Jenna's mother ran a plastic surgery business and had breast implants herself. She said that she did not want Jenna to have any hang-ups about the way she looked. Jenna herself was quoted as saying,

> You've got to have breasts to be successful. Every other person you see on television has had implants. I just want to be happy with my body and I think having my breasts enlarged will give me more self-confidence.[9]

Psychology experts thought that the operation was a risky way to resolve this teenage anxiety. Jenna's parents said that she had grown up around the plastic surgery industry, and Jenna considered surgery a normal way to improve her looks. Her parents felt that Jenna was mature enough to make the decision. However, they said they would defer to the decision of a medical doctor. Jenna's doctor said that at age 16, she was not physically mature enough for the surgery. Jenna would have to wait until she was 18 or 19 years old to have it.

necessarily improve their self-esteem if their problems are emotional. Teens need to talk with their doctors about their expectations. They need to make sure they have realistic expectations and are going into surgery for the right reasons.

MAKING THE CHOICE

The decision as to whether or not a teen should have cosmetic surgery depends on their reasons and expectations. Arguments can be made for either side of this debate. But it depends on whether or not the surgery is fulfilling a whim or making a positive change.

As Dr. Dorothy Ratusny, a psychotherapist, states in "Bodies under Construction" in *Faze Magazine*,

> *Teens need to be really realistic with the fact that cosmetic surgery may be only one piece of many things that serve to improve aspects of themselves. There may be physical changes but the real change begins with who they are inside.*[10]

In 1998, high school student Linda Maez had her breasts enlarged so they would look the same as Pamela Anderson's.

Fourteen-month-old Quinn Sliment had his cleft palate repaired by plastic surgery.

THE BEST OF COSMETIC SURGERY

osmetic surgery owes many of its procedures and progress to reconstructive plastic surgery. Due to modern medicine and greater safety precautions in work and play, the need for reconstructive surgeries has decreased.

However, there are still many situations in which cosmetic surgery can help restore badly injured or disfigured people to a more normal life. These types of cosmetic procedures are the very best that the cosmetic surgery industry has to offer society.

FIXING WHAT WENT WRONG

In the past, people who were born with birth defects, such as cleft lip, cleft palate, or other deformities, were forced to live with them. These people were destined for a life of being stared at, hidden away, or, in some cases, placed in circus sideshows. Cosmetic and reconstructive surgery has been able to correct many of these birth defects. Children can be spared from teasing and may become more confident adults.

Even children with minor deformities benefit from reconstructive surgery. Ears that stick out can be pinned back, and large, disfiguring birthmarks can be

Cleft Lip and Cleft Palate

Two birth defects that are most often seen and corrected by reconstructive surgeons are the cleft lip and the cleft palate. Both conditions occur during the development of an embryo when these facial features do not grow together normally.

A cleft palate is an opening in the roof of the mouth. The two plates that create the roof of the mouth fail to grow together completely. A cleft lip is a gap in the upper lip. The lip has not grown together normally. Cleft lip may occur on one side or both sides of the upper lip. It is one of the most common birth defects, occurring in about one of every 1,000 births.

minimized. As Sullivan states in her book *Cosmetic Surgery*,

> *The rewards of attractiveness begin at birth. . . . To the extent that attractive children are treated as if they are more intelligent, honest, social, and natural leaders, they will have more opportunities to behave accordingly . . . and more opportunities to internalize this view of themselves.*[1]

In some cases, a minor cosmetic procedure done in childhood can have positive results. The child will look better, have a better self-image, and be treated more normally by peers and adults. With these procedures, children may be more confident. For this reason, insurance companies will

A Safer World

One reason that elective cosmetic surgery grew was because of the reduced need for reconstructive surgeries. With the arrival of automobiles and mechanized workplaces in the early 1900s, the number of accidents increased. People were sometimes left with disfiguring injuries. More experienced reconstructive surgeons were needed to repair those injuries.

However, as safety standards improved, these accidents became less common. Vehicles began to have better safety equipment. Laws were established for better safety in the workplace. As a result, there was a sharp decrease in the number of injuries.

Doctors who had specialized in reconstructive surgery were suddenly competing for less business. As a result, surgeons whose practices had depended on reconstructive surgery began to pursue the elective cosmetic surgery business. And they began advertising for patients to have elective procedures.

often pay for children to have these procedures. In adults, however, insurance companies may refuse to pay for the same procedures, saying that they are for purely cosmetic reasons. According to Bethanne Snodgrass, "In many cases these deformities are corrected for the purpose of improving the child's appearance and social integration rather than for any functional need."[2]

Many people who have cosmetic surgery suffer from conditions that make them appear different from regular people. They want to look normal and not stand out in a crowd.

Lightening the Load

Many cosmetic procedures can improve a patient's quality of life. Breast reduction surgery, in which the size of the patient's breasts is surgically reduced, is done on both women and men. While this might seem like a purely cosmetic procedure, it can improve a patient's mental and physical health. Girls and women with large breasts are often subject to teasing. For boys who suffer from enlarged breasts, the teasing can be even worse.

Large breasts can also cause back pain and physical discomfort. Many insurance companies will

Marwa Naim received facial reconstructive surgery after an injury by a missile blast in her home in northern Baghdad in 2003.

pay for surgery to decrease the size of the breasts. Some critics argue that health reasons are being used falsely to justify this surgery. Others think it is important that breast reductions be treated as medical conditions. According to Deborah Sullivan,

> *Breast reduction . . . is presented at least partly as a treatment for health problems. Articles suggest it will cure neck and back pain, premenstrual tenderness, shoulder ache, nerve injury, bleeding and scarring from the pressure of bra straps, and rashes and infections caused by heavy breasts rubbing against underlying skin.*[3]

Many people who have the surgery feel that it relieves their physical symptoms and improves their outlook. They also feel relieved because they are more normally proportioned.

Help Is Available

Although the cost of cosmetic surgery has decreased and is more accessible to ordinary people, it is still too costly for many low-income families. Several organizations help provide surgeries for people who cannot afford surgery on their own. These groups work both in the United States and overseas.

A program known as Operation Smile is one of these services. Operation Smile sends teams of medical volunteers to other countries, where they treat children with deformities. During their stay, doctors usually examine 300 to 500 children. They then perform cosmetic surgery procedures on approximately 100 to 150 of them. The procedures include repairing

Weight-loss Surgery

Another surgical procedure that is considered both cosmetic and an important medical tool is weight-loss surgery. Cosmetic weight-loss surgery includes liposuction and tummy tucks. These body-contouring surgeries can impact how patients feel about themselves and their bodies, especially if they have already worked hard to lose weight. Weight-loss surgery can help overweight people reach a healthy weight. Being overweight can cause serious health problems for many people.

cleft lips, cleft palates, burns, tumors, and other injuries or defects.

Operation Smile founders Kathleen and William Magee recognize that some children with facial deformities will retreat from society. The only way to correct these deformities is through surgery. Operation Smile gives these children "an opportunity to come out of hiding and become active members of their community."[4]

Other similar medical service organizations include Austin Smiles and the Small World Foundation, among others.

"Defective" Children

Some cultures, such as the ancient Greeks, feared disfigured or imperfect children. They believed these children were evil or the result of something the mother did or saw during her pregnancy. They might place "defective" children on waste heaps outside of town. The children would die from exposure or be killed by wild animals.

From Positive to Negative

Cosmetic surgery can benefit many people who have suffered from deformities. However, most of the cosmetic procedures done in the United States today are performed on patients who want to improve their already normal looks. Cosmetic surgery has become more accepted and popular. As the demand for these services has increased, a darker side of the industry has emerged.

Michelle Comeau was left with multiple scars after she was stabbed by her boyfriend. She is now a candidate for cosmetic surgery by surgeon Dr. Julian Henley.

Angela Bismarchi has had 42 elective plastic surgery procedures.

THE PRICE OF COSMETIC SURGERY

Many people have benefited from cosmetic surgery. However, cosmetic surgery procedures are not foolproof. The procedures do not always have perfect results. Some patients have suffered life-threatening complications or even death from complications of cosmetic surgery.

The Cosmetic Surgery Gold Mine

Part of the reason for the increase in cosmetic surgery among consumers is the result of advertising by doctors, cosmetic surgery spas, and clinics. Cosmetic surgery is a well-paid business. As early as the 1930s, doctors discovered that they could make large amounts of money from these procedures. In cosmetic surgery, doctors do not have to wait for a patient to have a problem or illness. Cosmetic surgery is a choice.

In the 1960s and the 1970s, with increased health and safety standards, the number of people requiring reconstructive surgery had declined. Doctors specializing in cosmetic surgery began to seek patients for elective procedures through advertising. According to Sullivan,

Media Images

The media present the public with altered images of what the perfect face and body should look like. However, celebrities are usually wealthy enough to afford personal trainers, makeup artists, dieticians, and plastic surgeons. Many media images are also enhanced with computers. Computer retouching of photographs can make body parts appear slimmer or cover imperfections. Still, many people feel inadequate when they compare themselves to these images. Model Cindy Crawford once said in an interview, "Don't try to look like me. I don't even look like me."[1]

By 1988 a survey indicated that 48 percent of board-certified plastic surgeons advertised in the Yellow Pages and some advertised in newspapers, magazines, direct mail, television, and radio.[2]

With so much money to be made from elective cosmetic procedures, a number of less qualified medical professionals, some of them not even doctors, offered cheaper access to these procedures.

THE PRICE OF BEAUTY

In 2008, the cost for silicone breast implants was between $4,000 to $8,000. A face-lift could cost between $6,500 and $9,000. Liposuction costs ranged between $2,500 and $10,000, depending on the size of the area.

Most cosmetic procedures are not covered by medical insurance. Cosmetic surgeries are not thought to be necessary to a patient's health. Therefore, the consumer usually pays for the complete cost of the surgery. For this reason, many cosmetic surgeons have developed their own

Average Costs

In 2007, the average costs for plastic surgery procedures in the United States were:

- Botox injection: $380 per area
- Breast augmentation (saline): $3,690
- Breast augmentation (silicone): $4,087
- Eyelid tuck: $2,840
- Face-lift: $6,792
- Laser hair removal: $387
- Liposuction: $2,920
- Nose surgery: $4,357
- Tummy tuck: $5,350

Mauikai Gold traveled to Colombia where she had nose and breast surgery as well as full-body liposuction done.

financing and payment plans. This helps patients pay for the costly procedures.

However, another level of medical experts has also entered the field. They offer the same services for much lower rates than certified physicians. These doctors are often less experienced. According to Bethanne Snodgrass in *The Makeover Myth*,

> It is not at all difficult for an unqualified physician to set up shop to offer everything from skin-care advice to cosmetic

surgery. . . . It is common to find clinics, medical spas, day spas, and even beauty salons where nonphysicians perform medical procedures without physician supervision.[3]

As a result, patients can have major, invasive surgery performed by someone who is not qualified to do it. Patients may see poor results from their surgeries. They may also receive poor care or suffer dangerous side effects.

Insurance and Cosmetic Surgery

Health insurance generally covers only cosmetic procedures that are medically necessary. Many nose surgeries are covered by insurance if the patient has a deviated septum that makes breathing difficult or has frequent sinus infections. Breast reductions are often covered if they will get rid of chronic back pain. Many procedures for young children, such as pinning back large ears, are also paid for because of the effect they have on the child's emotional well-being. But most elective procedures done for cosmetic reasons are not covered by health insurance.

Some accredited doctors attend weekend seminars for extra training in cosmetic surgery. However, most of these doctors have not studied the procedures in depth. They may perform surgeries, such as face-lifts, without formal training. Some doctors perform these surgeries simply for more income. Without special training and experience in plastic surgery, these doctors also may fail to properly screen their patients. The doctors may not be aware of conditions that should make the patient ineligible for cosmetic procedures.

In the interest of saving money, some patients go overseas. Cosmetic surgery may be part of a vacation package tour to a foreign country. However, other countries do not regulate cosmetic surgery as tightly as the United States. Patients have an increased risk of infection due to the presence of unusual bacteria in other countries.

Cosmetic devices and products may differ from those used in the United States. For example, paraffin and industrial-grade silicone are often used in Latin American surgeries. These materials have been outlawed in the United States.

Sometimes U.S. doctors perform cosmetic surgeries

The Benefits of Medical Tourism

While there are horror stories about medical tourism, it can make basic health care more affordable for U.S. patients. Foreign doctors may offer health care at a much lower cost. It is estimated that more than 100,000 U.S. citizens travel abroad for cosmetic surgery every year. But others are now leaving the country for procedures that are medically necessary as well.

According to Dr. Matt Fontana of Global-Choice Healthcare, a medical tourism booking company,

> The medical tourism model has really been turned around as the health care crisis looms larger and larger. People are saying, "I'll pick the procedure and then I'll pick the destination."[4]

Sparrow Mahoney is a creator of a Web site for finding and comparing medical tourism options. According to Mahoney, "This isn't just getting a better nose job and going to the beach afterwards. This is really opening doors to Americans that have been shut for a long time."[5]

in other countries. But according to Snodgrass, "There are plenty of patients for doctors in the United States, and an expatriate surgeon may well be someone who has lost the ability to work legally at home."[6]

It Is Real Surgery

Like any surgery, cosmetic surgery carries the risk of side effects and complications. Although cosmetic surgery has become more common, patients need to understand that it still carries risks. Anyone having a procedure must be prepared for the possibility of complications or an unexpected result. Side effects can include minor swelling, bruising, infections, bleeding, skin discoloration, scars, blood clots, and heart and lung problems. With these possibilities in mind, patients need to decide if the procedure is worth the cost of the possible side effects.

Media Body Image

According to a University of California at Los Angeles article on body image, "Twenty-five years ago the average female model weighed 8% less than the average American woman. Currently, the average female model weighs 23% below [the American woman's] average weight. Only 5% of women have the genetic makeup to ever achieve the ultra-long and thin model body type so pervasive in the media."[7]

National Organization for Women President Kim Gandy speaks about the dangers of surgical implants.

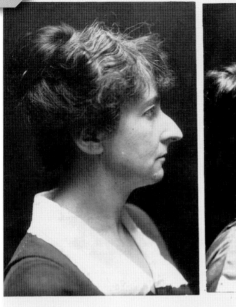

Before and after pictures of plastic surgery were sometimes published to show successful procedures.

The Cosmetic Surgery Experience

*I*t is difficult to make an informed decision about cosmetic surgery. Is it a good choice or a bad choice on a personal level and for society overall? Consider the stories of people who have had cosmetic surgery.

Very little was reported about the first people to have cosmetic surgery. Sometimes, doctors would publish stories of their patients. These were intended to make the surgeries sound simple and painless. They also emphasized the results. A *Good Housekeeping* article in 1940 shows how the personal story was used:

> *She was just a rather untidy girl with a big nose, sitting in the doctor's waiting room. A dusty felt hat pulled down over her eyes, her dowdy dress, and the way she slumped in the chair indicated her indifference to the details of her appearance. . . . Just four weeks later: the same girl—but how hard to recognize! Everything about her bespoke a touching new-born vanity. This miracle had followed a brief five days in the hospital, where skilled surgical hands had trimmed down her nose to pleasant proportions.*[1]

Today, Web sites for cosmetic surgery offer success stories from

Considering Cosmetic Surgery

A survey conducted by Plastic Surgery Research measured Americans' attitudes toward cosmetic surgery in 2008. The study found that only a little more than half of respondents approved of cosmetic surgery. As far as considering cosmetic surgery for themselves, 31 percent of women and 20 percent of men would consider surgery.

Breast Implant Controversy

The most widely publicized controversy in cosmetic surgery concerned the use of silicone breast implants. First introduced in 1963, these implants were often used until the 1980s. Silicone implants have numerous side effects. Side effects include scars, infection, displacement, leakage, and ruptures. The implants also interfere with breast-feeding and mammograms.

It was not until 1992 that the Food and Drug Administration banned the use of silicone breast implants. There have been widespread lawsuits against the Dow Corning Wright Company, its inventors, and the manufacturers from women whose health has been damaged by these implants. These women report health issues, such as ruptured implants, that require the removal of silicone from chests and armpits. They also report cancers and immune system disorders.

people who are thrilled with the outcomes. But by looking a little deeper, the voices of people who are not as happy with their decisions can be found.

BREAST SURGERIES

Patients who have breast surgery are often either thrilled with the results or wish they had never decided to have the procedure.

Some women suffer from constant back pain due to large breasts. They may also feel that they are out of proportion. According to one woman's story, the surgery went smoothly and she experienced minimal discomfort. She said, "I love the way I look! I had been having back problems for six years and was taking medication daily. . . . My self esteem and confidence in myself has taken a 360-degree turn. I feel so much better about myself and my appearance."[2] For this woman,

Some patients experience problems with implants and have them removed.

cosmetic surgery was not only important for her appearance, but also for health reasons.

Kim, another woman who posted her story online, had breast surgery. She found the procedure to be painful. She was swollen and bruised afterward. Though she initially enjoyed her new look, it did not last: "About 3 months after the original surgery one of the [breast] implants started to deflate. I noticed a size difference over a period of weeks."[3] Shortly after, several women in her family developed breast cancer. Many women cannot self-diagnose for signs

**A New Nose
in 40 Minutes**

In 1937, *Popular Science
Monthly* magazine ran an
article entitled "A New
Nose in 40 Minutes."
The photo essay detailed
the transformation of an
"unshapely" nose in a
way that would "change
the owner's face com-
pletely." It was one of the
first instances of cosmetic
surgery performed for the
media.

of breast cancer after having breast implants. Kim had the implants removed. Of her experience, she says, "I want to tell this story so that other women would learn from my mistake."[4]

NEW NOSES

Another common cosmetic surgery is the nose job. Like breast surgeries, the results can be positive or negative. A 16-year-old girl who had surgery to make her nose smaller was delighted with the results:

> *The procedure itself is relatively painless—I was knocked out. The following week was a little difficult. I could not go out because I was all bandaged up and my nose was extremely itchy. They also put packing in my nose which gets removed two days later. That was the worst part of it. Otherwise, once the bandages were off I felt and looked fine. I would recommend this procedure to anyone who is uncomfortable with their nose.*[5]

Unfortunately, others have been dissatisfied with the same procedure. A 15-year-old girl shares the story of her procedure:

> *The results were nothing short of horrifying. I looked like a burn victim; there was no definition in my nose—it looked like a blob of clay on my face. Worse still, the outer skin of my nostrils has pulled back leaving the openings extremely large, round and uneven.*[6]

This patient has had another corrective surgery since the first nose job. She will need to have a third surgery, in which her nose has to be rebroken. The total cost of all these procedures will be more than $11,000.

Smile Stories

There are many heartwarming stories of children

A Feminist Perspective

In her blog "LonerGrrrl," a woman named Michelle from the United Kingdom expresses her view of cosmetic surgery:

I abhor Western culture's obsession with cosmetic surgery. I detest the pressure placed on women to have their bodies cut open by a male surgeon's knife, more often than not their natural fat being sucked out only to be replaced by alien and unnatural substances like saline, just so they can fit a homogenous, profitable definition of beauty. I hate that these dangerous, bloody and expensive "procedures" are presented as a common sense "solution" to "fixing" a "problem" with a woman's appearance. Cosmetic surgery is one indicator of how modern-day Western women are still owned, controlled and hurt by the patriarchy. Women are not liberated when they are laid out on the table, being torn open by male hands, in order to boost his profit margins and conform to the male gaze's expectations of her.[7]

with birth defects who have had surgery and had improvements in their quality of life. One of these success stories is Brigid from Kenya, who was helped by the Operation Smile organization:

> *I was born with a cleft lip in Kaptrit, a small village in western Kenya. My parents didn't know that the repair of my lip was possible, and many of the children in our village were afraid of me. When I was 13, my family learned from our neighbor that Operation Smile doctors would be providing surgery in Nakuru. Now, the children in my village not only accept me, they believe I hold some kind of magic. I have more friends than ever.* [8]

By reading true stories from people who have had cosmetic surgery procedures, it is easier to see both the benefits and the drawbacks. Their stories show how these procedures have turned out for real people. As with any surgery, the outcome may not always be what the patient expects. This information is important in helping some people decide whether or not to have surgery.

Cindy McCain, wife of former presidential candidate John McCain, arranged for eleven-year-old Le Thi Phuoc to receive surgery by Operation Smile's doctors to repair a cleft lip.

Mary McDonough speaks on the dangers of cosmetic surgery.

WHEN NOT TO HAVE SURGERY

osmetic surgery has many benefits in the right situation. However, there are some very good reasons why cosmetic surgery is not always a good idea.

THE FEMINIST DEBATE

Many feminists have spoken out against cosmetic surgery since it began. They believe that women should not alter their looks to meet society's standard of beauty. Rather, women should work to change society's attitudes toward appearance. Society's standard of beauty contributes to many people's negative self-images. It also contributes to racism, sexism, and classism.

Fashion Trends

Like fashions, trends in what features are considered beautiful change over time. Even skin colors are subject to trends. For example, Caucasian women once struggled to keep their complexions fair, until fashion promoted tanned skin. There is always the possibility that a cosmetic procedure that is done for today's ideal will look out of place in the future.

An article in *Ms. Magazine* points out that cosmetic surgery practitioners use the image of a strong woman making her own choices as a basis for electing to have these procedures done:

> *The cosmetic surgery industry is . . . repackaging and reselling the feminist call to empower women into what may be dubbed "consumer feminism." . . . [They] are selling elective surgery as self-determination.* [1]

This viewpoint suggests that one of the worst reasons for someone to have cosmetic surgery is because another person wants it.

Many teens are unhappy with their appearance. But if they seek cosmetic surgery, it is important that they do not have unreasonable expectations.

PSYCHOLOGICAL FACTORS

There are many other potential red flags when it comes to cosmetic surgery and the patient's well-being. Patients must be mentally healthy if they decide to have cosmetic surgery. They must also have realistic expectations.

One common problem is when potential patients have unrealistic expectations for their surgeries. They may expect surgery to improve more than just their looks. They may expect to be happier, more loved, or more successful. However, surgery cannot solve these problems.

Some people suffer from body dysmorphic disorder. People with this disorder focus on a particular part of their body as being flawed. This flaw is usually imagined and that body part is perfectly normal. A person suffering from this disorder will not benefit from cosmetic surgery. They may, however, be desperate to have any kind of procedure that will correct the supposed flaw. Even with surgery, the disorder still exists in the patient's mind. The patient will continue to see the flaw no matter what is done. It is estimated that between 2 and 15 percent of people who seek cosmetic surgery may suffer from this disorder. Should they have cosmetic surgery, it may lead to psychological problems afterward.

Some people become addicted to surgical cosmetic procedures. They have surgery more often than most people. They always need something else

Paying for Cosmetic Surgery

As cosmetic surgery has risen in popularity, payment options have expanded. Since most cosmetic surgery is not covered by health insurance, the patient must pay the entire cost. Some providers have their own financing plans. Other patients turn to financing companies that specialize in cosmetic surgery loans. They may also get traditional bank loans to pay these costs. These loans can add to existing school loans, car loans, and mortgages and increase a patient's personal debt.

to be changed. As Virginia L. Blum, author of *Flesh Wounds: The Culture of Cosmetic Surgery*, wrote of cosmetic surgery addicts,

> *Surgery provides only temporary relief for feelings of emptiness and dissatisfaction. After each surgery, even if patients are happy for a while, they will soon find another part of their body they want to "improve."*[2]

Surgeons need to screen patients who continue to seek out surgeries to make sure they are not addicted to cosmetic surgery.

In addition, patients who are not satisfied with the results of their surgery may become upset or confused by the poor results. As Bethanne Snodgrass states in *The Makeover Myth*, "Some patients hope for dramatic changes in their lives that do not materialize. . . . When [these changes do] not occur, they sink into depression."[3]

Where Are the Surgeries Performed?

Where are cosmetic surgery procedures done in the United States? In 2007, 54 percent of cosmetic surgeries were done in an office setting. Seventeen percent of surgeries were performed in hospitals. Twenty-eight percent of cosmetic procedures were performed in nonhospital centers or clinics.

Sometimes even successful surgeries can have a negative impact on patients' lives. Patients may get attention they did not expect, such as family members or friends who feel uncomfortable with their new look. If the surgery altered a trait that runs in their family or one that is a sign of belonging to a particular cultural group, they may encounter tension within their families. They may regret having changed that feature. Another example is women who have breast implants and get more attention from men than they are used to. This attention may be unwanted and it can make the woman uncomfortable with her new body.

There are warning signs that qualified surgeons should look for when screening patients. These signs may indicate that the person is not psychologically fit to have cosmetic surgery at that time. These signs include impatience when a procedure cannot be done immediately or the desire to change a body part that seems normal. Doctors also interview patients to see if they are experiencing a life crisis. They try to find out if patients expect the procedure to help save a relationship, lead to more friends, or get a better job. Some patients may also be asking to have something done that another doctor has told them is unwise.

PHYSICAL FACTORS

Cosmetic surgery is often major surgery. It can have serious or even deadly side effects. Deaths caused by cosmetic surgery can be difficult to determine. Many are listed as heart attacks or respiratory failures. But in 2000, the *Plastic and Reconstructive Surgery* journal reported that one death occurred for every 5,000 liposuctions. Twenty people died for every 100,000 cosmetic surgeries. Other side effects

The Florida Story

In *The Makeover Myth*, Bethanne Snodgrass relates the story of a woman who awoke from cosmetic surgery in a clinic, alone and in medical distress:

In the darkness of an early Florida morning one April, a cab driver encountered a frightening sight. Collapsed on the sidewalk near a cosmetic surgery clinic was the body of a woman wearing a bloody garment and tangled in a web of intravenous tubing and monitor wires. The driver called the police and the woman was taken to a hospital, where she spent five days in intensive care. The woman later recounted that she had awakened in the fifth floor clinic gasping for breath but unable to find anyone to come to her aid. Too weak to walk, she dragged herself to the elevator and eventually into the street where she was found at 3:30 A.M.[4]

The woman was a victim of a cosmetic procedure done in a clinic without proper supervision. This is one of the greatest concerns of the medical community as cosmetic surgery becomes cheaper and more accessible.

include brain damage, blood clots, chronic pain, scarring, infection, and temporary paralysis. Cosmetic surgeries are not risk free and often have unexpected physical results.

Patients also need to consider that the results of most cosmetic surgeries are temporary. Face-lifts, eyebrow lifts, and tummy tucks do not last forever. They may need to be redone. The process of redoing cosmetic surgery can become costly over time. In addition, having multiple surgeries increases the health risks associated with them, especially as patients age.

The Bottom Line

There are many things for patients to think about when considering cosmetic surgery. If they decide that a procedure is the right step for them, then it is important to make the right choices. They must decide where they will have that procedure and who will

Longevity

How long does the average face-lift procedure last before it needs to be redone? With a healthy lifestyle, a face-lift may last for ten years. But that is without alcohol use or tobacco use, and with limited sun exposure. Heredity also plays a role in how long it will be before the signs of aging reappear. In a few cases, the effects of a face-lift may be permanent. But most people find that the procedure will have to be repeated in the future to maintain the same appearance.

The Plastic Surgery Channel

The makemeheal.com Web site has launched a cable television channel devoted to plastic surgery. The channel features six television shows that discuss all aspects of cosmetic surgery. Viewers can ask plastic surgeons questions through video chat software. The channel also intends to include more shows. These would include a celebrity plastic surgery gossip show, a daily news show, and a reality show that would follow real people through their plastic surgery experiences.

do it. How consumers and society approach those choices will dictate the future of cosmetic surgery in the United States.

Patients who have cosmetic surgery risk serious complications.

Those considering cosmetic surgery should consult with their doctors to decide if it is a good option for them.

MAKING THE
RIGHT CHOICE

For some people, cosmetic surgery makes a difference in their self-image and how they are accepted by society. For others, it may be a symptom of an unhealthy focus on looks. Having cosmetic surgery may also indicate the hope that by fixing their bodies, they will fix everything else that is wrong in their lives as well.

For those who decide that cosmetic surgery is right for them, what steps can be taken to ensure that they will have the best experience and the best results possible?

SURGERY CHECKLIST

Potential patients for cosmetic surgery must follow certain steps to make sure they will get the best possible care from a plastic surgeon. Many people approach cosmetic surgery casually. As Dr. Rod Rohrich states,

> *In America, most people spend more time finding the right pair of shoes than they do finding a cosmetic plastic surgeon. You can take back your shoes, but you can't take your face or your life back.* [1]

Patients must take responsibility for their care. They must be honest with their doctors about their medical history. They must tell doctors about any problems they have with medication, psychological issues, and substance abuse. They also need to be honest about their expectations for the surgery. The doctor needs this information to decide if the patients are good candidates for cosmetic procedures.

Potential patients must also research their doctors or cosmetic surgery providers. They need to make sure the doctors have good credentials and a good record of previous surgeries. Some spas and clinics do not have licensed doctors on staff. Patients have to decide if they are comfortable in a spa or clinic that does not have a doctor.

Patients also need to become familiar with the different procedures and instruments used in cosmetic surgery. This knowledge enables a patient to make informed decisions.

People who are considering cosmetic surgery must do their homework. As Bethanne Snodgrass states in *The Makeover Myth*, there are four basic steps:

❖ Get information from more than one source.

❖ Do not rely on ads. Check your doctor's credentials and record.

❖ Be skeptical until you have enough information.

❖ Take your time. Do not make decisions until you are informed and psychologically prepared.

For patients unsure about whether they want to have cosmetic surgery, computer-imaging software can create a picture of what the patient might look like after surgery. The patient's picture is digitally manipulated to show the possibilities and help the surgeon and patient decide the best treatment. Computer imaging can provide a patient with an approximation of their appearance after surgery. However, it cannot show exactly what a person will look like after surgery. The results may not always be as expected.

AVOIDING THE COSMETIC SURGERY TREND

Many people never even consider cosmetic surgery. They do not think that looks are very important. Some people have a good self-image and are able to accept aging as a natural part of life. Still others think that the risks of surgery are too great. They

Cosmetic Surgery in the Movies

Cosmetic surgery transformations are often featured in movies. In the early 1947 Humphrey Bogart movie *Dark Passage*, Bogart's character has surgery to change his identity and escape law enforcement. The movies *Seconds*, *Vanilla Sky*, and *Gattaca* also feature cosmetic surgery. In *Face/Off* with John Travolta, a police officer could take on the appearance of a criminal to track him down and infiltrate his organization. In every movie, the process of transformation always causes unexpected problems for the characters that have the surgery.

might try to maintain youthful looks through healthy living.

Anyone can take steps to avoid some of the signs of aging that cosmetic surgery is so ready to treat. Limiting sun exposure decreases the chances of getting skin cancer. It also keeps skin looking younger longer. Smoking is bad for overall health and the skin in particular. Smoking reduces blood supply to the skin. This results in skin having a grayish color. Most smokers look older than they are.

Exercise and a balanced diet also improve one's overall health and appearance. Limiting alcohol consumption and controlling weight are good health habits. These habits also help keep bodies youthful. In addition, it is important to get enough sleep, reduce stress, and stay mentally active.

These habits can help people avoid the signs of aging and make them happier and healthier. For people who have psychological issues regarding their appearance, counseling and therapy may be the only way to address the problems of self-image.

The Future of Cosmetic Surgery

As the popularity of cosmetic surgery increases every year, new procedures are constantly being developed. In November 2005, a team of French surgeons successfully performed the world's first partial face transplant on a woman who had been severely mauled by her dog. She was given a new nose, mouth, and chin from a deceased donor. Although the surgery had never been attempted before, it was successful at restoring the patient to a normal appearance. The doctor in charge of the surgery, Dr. Jean-Michel Dubernard, told the *New York Times* that he had already asked for permission to perform five more of these surgeries in the future. "We want to launch these new techniques to give hope to other people all over the world."[2]

Cosmetic surgeons are trying

Imperfections

In 2004, the United Kingdom *Daily Mail* reported that the rate of abortions in England had skyrocketed. This increase was reported as the result of women aborting fetuses that were identified as imperfect. Many abortions were performed when tests indicated deformities. However, many of these deformities were not life threatening, such as cleft lip, cleft palate, deformed feet, or even Down syndrome. According to the article,

. . . in 2002, 1,863 babies were aborted for reasons of suspected "deformity"—an eight percent increase over the previous 1,722 aborted in 2001, whereas Down's Syndrome abortions were up by 17 percent from 591 in 2001 to 691 in 2003.[3]

Ethics researchers say that society is trying to eliminate any defective members. They worry this attitude will decrease the tolerance for people with disabilities as a whole.

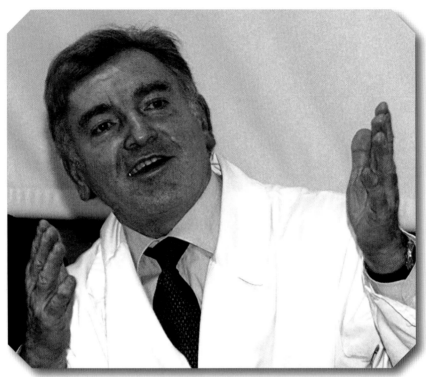

French surgeon Dr. Jean-Michel Dubernard performed the world's first partial face transplant.

to use less invasive procedures and fewer incisions. They are performing minor procedures on younger patients to forestall the signs of aging. Cosmetic surgeons may even begin using patients' DNA to formulate individual skin care products and makeup. Some surgeons hope to one day use a patient's stem cells in sculpting body parts and filling in wrinkles.

The demand for cosmetic surgery procedures is expected to increase as the age of the U.S. population increases. Baby boomers are the most likely age group to seek cosmetic surgery to minimize the signs of aging. Experts predict the demand for cosmetic procedures to increase by 19 percent from 2001 to 2010. They also expect unrealistic claims about new procedures and products to increase, as well as unethical and unsafe treatments.

SELF-IMAGE

Is cosmetic surgery beneficial to society? Or does it put too heavy an emphasis on looks? Is cosmetic surgery a healthy way to deal with flaws in one's appearance?

The issue of whether cosmetic surgery is a positive or negative aspect of today's culture comes down to individual circumstances and personal beliefs. For some people,

Mommy's Plastic Surgery

The children's book *My Beautiful Mommy* was published in 2008. Written by Dr. Michael Salzhauer, this picture book intended to help kids deal with any fears they might have when their mother has cosmetic surgery. The book has received a great deal of negative attention in the media. However, Salzhauer insists, "The intention is to allow parents who are going through this process anyway to have a vehicle to explain it to their kids."[4]

Plastic Surgery Statistics Worldwide

The most cosmetic surgeries are performed in Switzerland, with 214 surgeries every year per 100,000 people. India has the fewest, at only 0.209 procedures per 100,000 people. The United States averages 30 procedures annually per 100,000 people.

it is a tool to use to stay competitive or to achieve healthy self-image. For others, cosmetic surgery means accepting other people's standards of beauty, and to do so is to have an unhealthy self-image. Individuals have to make informed decisions about the place that cosmetic surgery has in their lives.

Body image sometimes affects whether or not a person chooses to have cosmetic surgery.

TIMELINE

600 BCE

1827

1914

The oldest known surgical reconstruction of noses and ear lobes occurs.

The first cleft palate corrective surgery is performed in the United States.

World War I creates a need for new reconstructive surgery techniques.

1960

1960s

1963

The Twilight Zone airs an episode titled, "The Eye of the Beholder."

The first breast augmentation surgeries are performed.

Silicone breast implants are first introduced.

1921

The American Association of Plastic Surgeons is organized.

1923

Actress Fanny Brice has a rhinoplasty. She is the first celebrity to publicly announce her cosmetic surgery procedure.

1931

Dr. J. Howard Crum performs a public face-lift before a convention crowd in New York City.

1968

A group of young women gather to protest the Miss America pageant and the ideal of the perfect woman.

1984

Singer Michael Jackson is assumed to have had his first cosmetic surgery on his nose.

1990

Artist Orlan has her first cosmetic surgery performance art procedure.

TIMELINE

1991

Kathleen and William Magee found Operation Smile to perform reconstructive surgery on poor children.

1992

The use of silicone breast implants is severely restricted due to concerns over heath issues in women who had received them.

2002

Extreme Makeover premieres on television.

2005

The world's first partial face transplant is performed in France.

2001

Jenna Franklin makes headlines when her parents agree to give her breast augmentation surgery for her sixteenth birthday.

2002

The FDA approves Botox injections for use in filling facial wrinkles.

2007

Surgical and nonsurgical procedures performed annually in the United States reach 11.7 million.

2008

My Beautiful Mommy, a children's book about cosmetic surgery, is published.

ESSENTIAL FACTS

AT ISSUE

Opposed

❖ The cosmetic surgery industry perpetuates an unattainable image of beauty as shown daily in the media and supports discrimination against people who are not considered beautiful.

❖ Cosmetic surgery procedures can have unexpected results and life-threatening complications.

❖ Cosmetic surgery will not necessarily change people's lives for the better.

In Favor

❖ Cosmetic surgery can make a difference for people with disfigurements or abnormalities caused by accidents or birth defects.

❖ For people with low self-esteem, or poor body image, cosmetic surgery can make a difference in how they feel about themselves.

❖ Cosmetic surgery has become less expensive and more affordable, making it available to more people.

CRITICAL DATES

1914–1918
World War I injuries forced doctors to pioneer many of the plastic surgery techniques now used for cosmetic surgery.

1921
The American Association of Plastic Surgeons was organized.

1923
Actress Fanny Brice was the first celebrity to publicly admit to having a nose job.

2005
The world's first partial face transplant was performed in France.

2007
The number of cosmetic surgery procedures done annually in the United States topped 11 million.

QUOTES

"The cosmetic surgery industry is . . . repackaging and reselling the feminist call to empower women into what may be dubbed 'consumer feminism.' . . . [They] are selling elective surgery as self-determination."—*Jennifer Cognard-Black*

"In a world where we are judged by how we appear, the belief that we can change our appearance is liberating. We are what we seem to be and we seem to be what we are!"—*Sander Gilman*

ADDITIONAL RESOURCES

SELECT BIBLIOGRAPHY

Etcoff, Nancy. *Survival of the Prettiest: The Science of Beauty*. New York: Anchor Books. 2000.

Haiken, Elizabeth. *Venus Envy: A History of Cosmetic Surgery*. Baltimore, MD: Johns Hopkins University Press. 1997.

Kuczynski, Alex. *Beauty Junkies: Inside Our $15 Billion Obsession with Cosmetic Surgery*. New York: Doubleday. 2006.

Snodgrass, Bethanne. *The Makeover Myth: The Real Story behind Cosmetic Surgery, Injectables, Lasers, Gimmicks, and Hype, and What You Need to Know to Stay Safe*. New York: HarperCollins. 2006.

Sullivan, Deborah A. *Cosmetic Surgery: The Cutting Edge of Commercial Medicine in America*. Piscataway, NJ: Rutgers University Press. 2001.

FURTHER READING

Alagna, Magdalena. *Everything You Need to Know about the Dangers of Cosmetic Surgery*. New York: Rosen Publishing Group. 2001.

Bailey, Kristin, ed. *At Issue: Cosmetic Surgery*. Farmington Hills, MI: Thomson Gale. 2005.

Redd, Nancy Amanda. *Body Drama: Real Girls, Real Bodies, Real Issues, Real Answers*. New York: Penguin Books. 2007.

Web Links

To learn more about cosmetic surgery, visit ABDO Publishing Company online at **www.abdopublishing.com**. Web sites about cosmetic surgery are featured on our Book Links page. These links are routinely monitored and updated to provide the most current information available.

For More Information

For more information on this subject, contact or visit the following organizations.

Love Your Body Foundation
P.O. Box 1848, Merrifield, VA 22116-8048
(202) 628-8669
http://loveyourbody.nowfoundation.org/
The foundation educates women about oppressive beauty standards and encourages women to have a healthy body image.

University of Iowa Hospitals and Clinics Medical Museum
200 Hawkins Drive, Iowa City, IA 52242
http://www.uihealthcare.com/depts/medmuseum/index.html
The museum has had exhibits about the cultural body and how different societies have encouraged body alterations and body painting.

University of Pennsylvania Museum of Archaeology and Anthropology
3260 South Street, Philadelphia, PA 19104
www.museum.upenn.edu
The museum has an online exhibit, "The Real Me: Therapeutic Narratives in Cosmetic Surgery," as well as on-site exhibits relating to the history of body modification in other cultures.

GLOSSARY

abdominoplasty
Often referred to as a "tummy tuck," the process of tightening loose abdominal skin.

anesthesia
Artificially induced unconsciousness that keeps a patient from feeling pain during an operation.

augmentation
The process of enlarging a body part, such as the breasts.

body contouring
Changing the shape and size of body features and the patient's overall appearance, using cosmetic surgery.

body dysmorphic disorder
A disease in which patients have a distorted image of their bodies or certain parts of their bodies.

Botox
A cosmetic made from botulin, which in small amounts can smooth facial lines and wrinkles.

collagen
A protein produced by cows that is used as a filler for lines and wrinkles.

cosmetic surgery
Reshaping healthy body structures to improve appearance.

elective surgery
Nonemergency surgical procedure that is optional and chosen by the patient.

implant
Something that is inserted or imbedded surgically to enhance part of the body.

invasive procedures
Procedures requiring incisions or surgery.

liposuction
Extracting fat from an area of the body using suction.

medical tourism
> Travel tours to foreign countries where patients can undergo less expensive medical procedures.

noninvasive procedures
> Procedures that do not require incisions.

paraffin
> A white, waxy substance that was once used as a body filler.

plastic surgery
> Repairing damaged body parts or forming new body structures to replace missing parts.

reconstructive surgery
> Improving body parts that are abnormal or damaged.

rhinoplasty
> Surgically reshaping or resizing the nose.

silicone
> A type of polymer used as a filler for breast augmentation surgeries.

SOURCE NOTES

Chapter 1. An Obsession with Looks
1. "Putting Your Best Face Forward," *Psychology Today*. New York: Sussex Publishers. May 2004.
2. Deborah A. Sullivan. *Cosmetic Surgery: The Cutting Edge of Commercial Medicine in America*. Piscataway, NJ: Rutgers University Press, 2004. 1.
3. Bethanne Snodgrass. *The Makeover Myth: The Real Story behind Cosmetic Surgery, Injectables, Lasers, Gimmicks, and Hype, and What You Need to Know to Stay Safe*. New York: HarperCollins, 2006. 5.
4. Christine Rosen. "The Democratization of Beauty." *The New Atlantis Journal of Technology and Society*. Spring 2004. 10.

Chapter 2. The Evolution of Cosmetic Surgery
1. Elizabeth Haiken. *Venus Envy: A History of Cosmetic Surgery*. Baltimore, MD: The Johns Hopkins University Press, 1997. 96.
2. Deborah A. Sullivan. *Cosmetic Surgery: The Cutting Edge of Commercial Medicine in America*. Piscataway, NJ: Rutgers University Press, 2004. 39.
3. Elizabeth Haiken. *Venus Envy: A History of Cosmetic Surgery*. Baltimore, MD: The Johns Hopkins University Press, 1997. 33.

Chapter 3. Cosmetic Surgery Explored
1. Jeremy Drummond. "Digibodies: Orlan." 10 July 2008 <http://www.digibodies.org/online/orlan.htm>.

Chapter 4. The Quest for Beauty
1. Deborah A. Sullivan. *Cosmetic Surgery: The Cutting Edge of Commercial Medicine in America*. Piscataway, NJ: Rutgers University Press, 2004. 8.
2. Bethanne Snodgrass. *The Makeover Myth: The Real Story behind Cosmetic Surgery, Injectables, Lasers, Gimmicks, and Hype, and What You Need to Know to Stay Safe*. New York: HarperCollins, 2006. 73.
3. Sander Gilman. *Making the Body Beautiful*. Princeton, NJ: Princeton University Press, 1999. 3.

Chapter 5. Teens and Cosmetic Surgery
1. Bethanne Snodgrass. *The Makeover Myth: The Real Story behind Cosmetic Surgery, Injectables, Lasers, Gimmicks, and Hype, and What You Need to Know to Stay Safe*. New York: HarperCollins, 2006. 237.
2. Elizabeth Haiken. *Venus Envy: A History of Cosmetic Surgery*. Baltimore, MD: The Johns Hopkins University Press, 1997. 91.

3. "Briefing Papers: Plastic Surgery for Teenagers." *American Society of Plastic Surgeons*. 2008. 10 July 2008 <http://www.plasticsurgery.org/ media/briefing_papers/Plastic-Surgery-for-Teenagers-Briefing-Paper.cfm>.

4. Paula Gray Hunker. "Pressure to be Perfect." *Insight on the News*. 13 Mar. 2000. 10 July 2008 <http://findarticles.com/p/articles/mi_ m1571/is_10_16/ai_60130264>.

5. Liane Beam Wansbrough. "Bodies under Construction." *Faze Magazine*. Fall 2003. 10 July 2008 <http://www.fazeteen.com/fall2003/ cosmeticsurgery.htm>.

6. "Briefing Papers: Plastic Surgery for Teenagers." *American Society of Plastic Surgeons*. 2008. 10 July 2008 <http://www.plasticsurgery.org/ media/briefing_papers/Plastic-Surgery-for-Teenagers-Briefing-Paper.cfm>.

7. Sandra G. Boodman. "For More Teenage Girls, Adult Plastic Surgery." *Washington Post*. 26 Oct. 2004. 11 Aug. 2008 <http://www. washingtonpost.com/wp-dyn/articles/A62540-2004Oct25_3.html>.

8. Tamar Nordenberg. "Kids and Cosmetic Surgery: Are Teens Too Young to Go Under the Knife?" *Discovery Health: Plastic Surgery*. 2008. 11 Aug. 2008 <http://health.discovery.com/centers/plasticsurgery/ general/plasticsurgery_kids.html>.

9. "Mother Defends Teenager's Breast Op." *BBC News Online: Health*. 4 Jan. 2001. 10 July 2008 <http://news.bbc.co.uk/2/low/ health/1100471.stm>.

10. Liane Beam Wansbrough. "Bodies under Construction." *Faze Magazine*. Fall 2003. 10 July 2008 <http://www.fazeteen.com/fall2003/ cosmeticsurgery.htm>.

Chapter 6. The Best of Cosmetic Surgery

1. Deborah A. Sullivan. *Cosmetic Surgery: The Cutting Edge of Commercial Medicine in America*. Piscataway, NJ: Rutgers University Press, 2004. 18.

2. Bethanne Snodgrass. *The Makeover Myth: The Real Story behind Cosmetic Surgery, Injectables, Lasers, Gimmicks, and Hype, and What You Need to Know to Stay Safe*. New York: HarperCollins, 2006. 235.

3. Deborah A. Sullivan. *Cosmetic Surgery: The Cutting Edge of Commercial Medicine in America*. Piscataway, NJ: Rutgers University Press, 2004.166.

4. Kathleen Magee and William Magee, "Operation Smile: Changing Lives, One Smile at a Time," *Reclaiming Children and Youth*, vol. 9, Fall 2000. 162.

SOURCE NOTES CONTINUED

Chapter 7. The Price of Cosmetic Surgery

1. Bethanne Snodgrass. *The Makeover Myth: The Real Story behind Cosmetic Surgery, Injectables, Lasers, Gimmicks, and Hype, and What You Need to Know to Stay Safe.* New York: HarperCollins, 2006. 32.

2. Deborah A. Sullivan. *Cosmetic Surgery: The Cutting Edge of Commercial Medicine in America.* Piscataway, NJ: Rutgers University Press, 2004. 138–139.

3. Bethanne Snodgrass. *The Makeover Myth: The Real Story behind Cosmetic Surgery, Injectables, Lasers, Gimmicks, and Hype, and What You Need to Know to Stay Safe.* New York: HarperCollins, 2006. 103–104.

4. Mark Repasky. "A Cut Below: Americans Look Abroad for Healthcare," *ABC News.com.* 29 Aug. 2006. 10 July 2008 <http://abcnews.go.com/Business/IndustryInfo/story?id=2320839&page=1>.

5. Ibid.

6. Bethanne Snodgrass. *The Makeover Myth: The Real Story behind Cosmetic Surgery, Injectables, Lasers, Gimmicks, and Hype, and What You Need to Know to Stay Safe.* New York: HarperCollins, 2006. 117.

7. UCLA SNAC (Student Nutrition & Body Image Action Committee). "Body Image." 10 July 2008 <http://www.snac.ucla.edu/pages/Body_Image/Body_Image.htm>.

Chapter 8. The Cosmetic Surgery Experience

1. Elizabeth Haiken. *Venus Envy: A History of Cosmetic Surgery.* Baltimore, MD: The Johns Hopkins University Press, 1997. 128–129.

2. "Talksurgery.com Personal Stories: No More Back Pain." Plastic Surgery Information Service. 14 Oct. 2008 <http://www.talksurgery.com/consumer/stories/story00000118.html>.

3. "Talksurgery.com Personal Stories: To the Boob Buyer, Beware!" Plastic Surgery Information Service. 10 July 2008 <http://www.talksurgery.com/consumer/stories/story00000248.html>.

4. Ibid.

5. "Talksurgery.com Personal Stories: Much Better." Plastic Surgery Information Service. 14 Oct. 2008 <http://www.talksurgery.com/consumer/stories/story00000060.html>.

6. "Talksurgery.com Personal Stories: All I Wanted Was a Straight Nose." Plastic Surgery Information Service. 14 Oct. 2008 <http://www.talksurgery.com/consumer/stories/story00000095.html>.

7. "A step forward, but we're still not getting very far," Lonergrrrl: Feminist Rants and Musings. 10 Sept. 2006. 4 Sept. 2008 <http://lonergrrrl.blogspot.com/2006/09/step-forward-but-were-still-not.html>.

8. "Smile Stories: Before and After Smiles: Kenya: Brigid." Operation Smile. 14 Oct. 2008 <http://www.operationsmile.org/testimonials/brigid/>.

Chapter 9. When Not to Have Surgery

1. Jennifer Cognard-Black. "Has Artificial Beauty Become the New Feminism?" *Ms. Magazine*. 29 Sept. 2007. 10 July 2008 <http://www.alternet.org/healthwellness/63683/>.

2. Virginia L. Blum, *Flesh Wounds: The Culture of Cosmetic Surgery*. Berkeley: University of California Press, 2003.

3. Bethanne Snodgrass. *The Makeover Myth: The Real Story behind Cosmetic Surgery, Injectables, Lasers, Gimmicks, and Hype, and What You Need to Know to Stay Safe*. New York: HarperCollins, 2006. 221.

4. Ibid. 99.

Chapter 10. Making the Right Choice

1. Bethanne Snodgrass. *The Makeover Myth: The Real Story behind Cosmetic Surgery, Injectables, Lasers, Gimmicks, and Hype, and What You Need to Know to Stay Safe*. New York: HarperCollins, 2006. 99.

2. Ariane Bernard and Craig S. Smith. "French Face-Transplant Patient Tells of Her Ordeal." *New York Times*. 7 Feb. 2006. 10 July 2008 <http://www.nytimes.com/2006/02/07/international/europe/07face.html>.

3. "British Abortion Rate Skyrockets as Couples Eliminate 'Defective' Children." *LifeSiteNews.com*. 31 May 2004. 10 July 2008 <http://www.lifesitenews.com/ldn/2004/may/04053105.html>.

4. "Kid's Book Explains Mommy's Plastic Surgery." *USA Today*. 17 Apr. 2008. 10 July 2008 <http://www.usatoday.com/news/health/2008-04-17-Plastic-surgery_N.htm>.

INDEX

ABOUT THE AUTHOR

Marcia Amidon Lusted is the author of more than a dozen books for children, as well as numerous magazine articles. She is also on the editorial staff of Cobblestone Publishing, in addition to her work as a writing instructor and a musician. She lives in New Hampshire with her husband and three sons.

PHOTO CREDITS

Yvonne Hemsey/Getty Images, cover, 42; Elizabeth Shoemaker/ iStock Photo, 6; Danny Moloshok/AP Images, 10; Leslie Mazoch/ AP Images, 15; AP Images, 16; Popperfoto/Getty Images, 19; Time & Life Pictures/Getty Images, 23; AFP/Getty Images, 24; Joe Kohen / AP Images, 29; Chiaki Stukumo/AP Images, 31; Damian Dovargane /AP Images, 32; Andreas Rentz/Getty Images, 41; Lauren Greenfield/AP Images, 47, 85; Paul Harris/Getty Images, 51; Tom Gannam/AP Images, 52; Nick Ut/AP Images, 56; Jack Sauer/AP Images, 59; Silbia Izquierdo/AP Images, 60; Phelan M. Ebenhack/AP Images, 63; Kevin Wolfe/AP Images, 67; Topical Press Agency/Getty Images, 68; Donna McWilliam/AP Images, 71; Hoang Dinh Nam/AFP/Getty Images, 75; Ron Edmonds/AP Images, 76; Ned Frisk Photography/Jupiterimages/AP Images, 78; Image Source/AP Images, 86, 95; Patrick Gardin/AP Images, 92